CAPABLE MONSTERS

CAPABLE MONSTERS

POEMS

MARLIN M. JENKINS

BULL CITY PRESS
DURHAM, NORTH CAROLINA

Capable Monsters

Published in the United States of America

Library of Congress Cataloging-in-Publication Data

Jenkins, Marlin M.
Capable Monsters: poems / by Marlin M. Jenkins
p. cm.
ISBN-13: 978-1-949344-12-7

Book design by Spock and Associates
Cover artwork by Maria Krutz
Author photo by Emma Richter

Published by
BULL CITY PRESS, LLC
1217 Odyssey Drive
Durham, NC 27713

www.BullCityPress.com

for my father who, when I asked, as a small child, if he thought charizard or blastoise was better, said he couldn't answer the question without more information

and for my mother, who, when asked, "if pokémon were real would you get me one?" said, "No"

and for Atatiana Jefferson

ENTRIES

where there be monsters whose teeth
are sharp and sparkle with lost

people. lost poems. who
among us can imagine ourselves
unimagined?

—**LUCILLE CLIFTON**, "here yet be dragons"

You humans are a dangerous species. You brought me into your world with no purpose but to be your slave. But now I have my own purpose.

—**MEWTWO**, *Pokémon: The First Movie*

I have a request of you…On the desk there is my invention, POKEDEX! It's a hi-tech encyclopedia!...Take [this] with you!

—**PROFESSOR OAK**, *Pokémon Red/Blue/Yellow Version*

EVOLUTION

I was a boy and then
I switched from milk.

I was a moth and then
a boy plucked the wings

and rubbed them into
freshly-sprouting stubble.

I was a stumbling block
and then

the wood cracked
straight through

and from the outside
you couldn't see the splinters.

I was a monster
and now

I am a monster
still

but with different teeth.

TALL GRASS

Boy-man whose breath is prayer
ready to breathe life
into video game cartridge.

Boy-man who don't eat lunch
at school if the lunch ain't free
this year, whose hunger

pastes eyes to closely-clutched
gray-scale screen all through church.
Boy-man proclaimed man

of the house—with second-hand clothes
from black garbage bag, used copy
of Pokémon Blue Version.

First chosen pokémon: bulbasaur—
pocket-monster with back-bulb
which grows like the dividing cells

mutating in granddad's lungs. Sprouting
ivy. Boy-man briefly second-guesses choice:
perhaps instead of bulbasaur

should have picked squirtle: shell
which would grow and sprout
water-cannons, defeat each enemy

through baptism. He learns
to deal, make do—like the bankruptcy,
like the block, like the non-profit boxes

that provided Christmas morning.
Boy-man whose bulbasaur provides
protection; he knows

from what he was told by the pokémon
professor you don't walk through
the tall grass without a pokémon,

like he knows from mother
you don't walk outside alone at night.
The boy-man and his new

green friend—bulbasaur who was
a bulbasaur until he wasn't: evolved
into ivysaur and the pre-plant

of sealed bulb became
flower, leaf, vine. And then, finally:
venusaur—titan with a tree

rooted to his back, the ability
to alter sunlight, channel
its energy. Boy-man wishes

himself this world of trouble
and wonder: cyber-world
where you battle until you can't

but all healing takes is one nurse
and six seconds—where
the tall grass grows and is never

cut down. If only he could be
more like a grown bulbasaur: enough
grown green to photosynthesize—

never be in hunger, always be in bloom.

POKÉDEX ENTRY #1: BULBASAUR

A strange seed was planted on its back at birth. The plant sprouts and grows with this Pokémon.

Root wrapped around spine,
          pre-flower, vine under bud,
what do we call what we carry
          on and in our backs,
                    what burns under our skin
          and ties itself to our nerves
and endings? I was born
          with bad blood and the makings
of napped hair and crackled skin
and all the things the doctor
                    makes me list: the family
          history of depression and addiction
          and cancer—and maybe there are
some patterns we can't break.
          Research says trauma
from our parents may live
                    in our DNA. The bulbous
nucleus at the center
          of each cell like a bulb
ready, dangerous, the sprouting collage
                    in each of us. I let
          my seed grow, sprout, open,
everything given to me
at birth: awesome and visible,
          my awful nourishment.

kindness

here: my throat
torn open
down the center.

the pull
of a frayed rope.

here: the rope
and the rope-
burn.

the rash
across my forehead—
do-rag tied too tight.
scraped the oil-filled
sacs with my nails.
would have used
teeth if i could. here:

the extra
buttons. the thin balloons
i used as lungs. please—
if i show you
where it hurts
don't say it will be
fine. i know
you are not a mind reader.
that's mostly
the point. here is

every crevice
where water

floods from me
when i sleep—
if i sleep.

i die and wake back up
in the same spot i was
killed and it repeats until
i forget what i think
dying feels like.

here is a vhs
that is all static.

torn pokémon
cards with demons
jumping from the mouths.

here is the altar,
the church, the steeple,
a needle, my empty.

here are
the pilot lights
i hide
in my nostrils.
please
come close
enough
that you
could blow
them out.

POKÉDEX ENTRY #4: CHARMANDER

From the time it's born, a flame burns at the tip of its tail. Its life would end if the flame were to go out.

As a charmander grows into the dragon-
winged charizard, this wick becomes
strong enough to force everyone away

if it wishes with a single swish. This ability to clear
any space with just your tail, let alone the fire
you breathe. How far is it from pilot-light

to core? How many times have you watched
the orange whimper in a storm or when sick?
Where do you lie still when the dread hits? When

the depression hits? Perhaps a mountainside or maybe
a cave you hide away in, sleep when the cooling isn't
always explainable. Sometimes the world is just

too much, and we lie alone and motionless, say
the cleared cavern is just where we go when
we need space, wait to become one

with the temperature of the room.

POKÉDEX ENTRY #7: SQUIRTLE

The shell is soft when it is born. It soon becomes so resilient, prodding fingers will bounce off it.

boy you soft you gay you ain't shit
you awkward ain't real fake-ass sad boy
oreo-ass goodie goodie know-it-all nerd
doin too much let us tell you 'bout yourself
we see your fear like how you sit by yourself
and tremble like how you think you too good
to have any friends like that time skating a boy
skated close tried to pass you and then by reflex
you blocked his swinging arm he looked at you
like your gay ass was trying to hold his hand

it is not that there is shell with me inside it
it is that i and shell are part and participle
compartmented coat to coax both poison
and antidote from how the phrases turn
i begun and i begin i be in this resilient
skin and all my clenched fingers ready
and all my sweat reflective and all my
shields sharpened and all my shell
a hardened rampage of rubber

some theories on origins

a pokémon can only say its name
or
it gets its name from the only thing
it can say

if the second case
then call me whine call me race
call me lonely monster nerdy trivia

from the time i was born i was
ready to know useless knowledge
to overthink an olive pit to obsess
and obsess repeat repeat

i was born and then soon
putting barrettes in my hair
climbing the tallest cabinets
to stuff cheerios in my diaper

i was born not with this language
with words for cereal or game or pixel
or pain

i grew and learned through symbols

gave my family
new names

left pallet town's square
of seclusion and there is much
the professor didn't tell me
about a world called kanto

about all the other regions
i could've flown to if i'd known

a visit home reveals to me
how i am a young version
of my shared-name father
we sit the same way
legs crossed stand the same way
with hands pressing the lower back
i noticed neither similarity
until it was said to me

when i was born
i did not know who my people were
and so i hated everyone who knew where
they belonged but hated more
everyone coated in a shiny mirror
everyone who wanted the best for me
everyone who chose me before
i could choose them

canon is unclear about who writes the pokédex
perhaps the professor notes from field work
before pallet town locked him in
a single room and each night
he stares into the mouth
of the river counting bubbles
and wishing each is a live creature

or is it just the adventuring child
jotting hyperbolic notes
while camped in the tall grass

maybe it's basically wikipedia with all
us trainers breeders battlers researchers

fashionistas filling in the legends
told to us from oral histories

ash asks the pokédex for nomenclature
it tells him what everything is
and he believes it

he calls his pikachu pikachu
and when pikachu responds:
pika pi pikachu the only lonely
vocabulary between his electric
cheeks red with innocence
he is saying *human human human*

i was born a human
if we start that basic
i was born and celebrate it
once a year i was born

and oh i remember i am thankful
and so i am sure to say i am thankful

my sisters call me not by my name
now it is brother
growing up it was just boy

a friend texts me calls me love
instead of my name
and i'm happy i was born
i was born in this skin
as this species and these
funny semi-fluid categories
and i learned i learned
these preoccupations this pain
this poking in my nerve endings

i was born and my name is not
what my mother
wanted to call me

in large crowds i think
i hear my name and i know not
what to say except
to shout it back

POKÉDEX ENTRY #778: MIMIKYU

A lonely Pokémon, it conceals its terrifying appearance beneath an old rag so it can get closer to people and other Pokémon.

i could kill a man
if he looks too close
without even touching him
take my word for it
once a lover tried
to look me in the eye
and died instantly   look
i don't mean to be this way
i was born and
that's when the problem started
or maybe that's the whole problem
i used to look in the mirror
every morning
and say boy
you are beautiful
three times
but my therapist says
i should stop lying to myself
look how i've drawn on this new face
look   i get it
i know what you like
i know what they all like
i know what they're all like
i know how your stomach
would turn
when trickles of toxic sweat
drip from my crooked fangs
i never meant to hurt
anyone   please   i know
what i am capable of   trust me

i know what i am
cotton and crayon covering
what i have cut and rearranged
cut and rearranged
i've had to teach myself to stitch
developed this palatable craft
come see the ragged details on the sheet

ALL THE BETTER

Boy / what big lies you have /
        What big lashes /

What large heaps to hide
        behind / cardboard and colored glass /

Boy / what grubby hands you have /
        What big histories / Boy lying

wet in his mother/'s
        bed / Boy now with a boy

in his bed / Boy who didn't play
        the boy when given a chance /

Boy with TV screens
        for eyes / with

pixeled frown / What big holes
        there are

in your memory / in your
        melody / in the ways

you rise from the sheets / alone /
        and do / and don't / see / a boy

POKÉDEX ENTRY #91: CLOYSTER

Even a missile can't break the spikes it uses to stab opponents. They're even harder than its shell.

i dreamt a calcified sculpture   fashioned from my own
intestines prodded   the bottom of the sea.
found a groove to finger.   found an eye-less beast.
found a detached shell   to hold upright.
as a child   i dreamt of swords
to carve an opening   for entrails to trail a path
out the front door.   i dream my fingers
sharpened and stone   on the ends of spears.
i am thankful   for the movement of blood
as its flow stays within   my callous body, thankful
for the man's shit-tipped   finger as it leaves me
split. do not enter   with your eyes.   there is a dark
cavern in me, waiting.   there is a spiked monster
there, protecting friend   whose sharp jostling
reminds me of how my own   cardiac current flows.
we bleed and keep the door   shut. we are both afraid of light.

POKÉDEX ENTRY #131: LAPRAS

People have driven Lapras almost to the point of extinction. In the evenings, this Pokémon is said to sing plaintively as it seeks what few others of its kind still remain.

You find yourself in a dark room where Drake and Snoop
and Kendrick play at a dance party you stumbled into
and again you hear *nigga* over white speakers and
uncomfortable only begins to explain how you feel
and you're the only Black person in the room
like you've been so often and people are trying to get you
to dance but you just want to leave shit you just want
to leave but they want you to dance they want you
to enjoy this on the anniversary of Michael Brown's
death on a day where you feel so few and wish to sing
the song of your own authentic and rugged and sweet
and this circle of people feels like circus ring
or maybe more like cage or maybe more like
a ring of thieves and you say to yourself it's just
music I mean it's just a birthday party I mean it's just
people having fun just the smell of booze and sweat
in a dark room where people are just people
and are just celebrating but that doesn't stop you
from feeling out of place and scared and profoundly
upset to say the least and you know your people keep
dying while your music plays at parties where before
you walked in there were no Black people
so you leave and go listen to your own rap music
from your own iTunes with your own headphones
on your own laptop to hear the songs
of us trying to remain to survive despite
to sing something to find each other again

POKÉDEX ENTRY #39: JIGGLYPUFF

When this Pokémon sings, it never pauses to breathe. If it is in a battle against an opponent that does not easily fall asleep, Jigglypuff cannot breathe, endangering its life.

i wished my words a lullaby
to calm a killer's readied claw
but found myself the tired one,
my mouth hung open: but what's worth
my breath if i am not willing
to die for it? of course this is
the wrong question: i've been willing
to die for less, but still—how dare
another take from us what's ours,
we who've been choked and yet have kept
singing. and yet. and yes, true, god
did bid me sing but in the same
breath did wish me death, and battle:
a birthright to sing until emptied.

POKÉDEX ENTRY #425: DRIFLOON → #426: DRIFBLIM

It is whispered that any child who mistakes Drifloon for a balloon and holds on to it could wind up missing
[evolves into] →
At dusk, swarms of them [Drifblim] are carried aloft on winds. When noticed, they suddenly vanish

I wake and have the same fingers. Same body. Same aimless

gravity holding a child with growing hands. Not all my mistakes

are mistakes. The hole I drilled in my bedroom wall

was not a mistake. I often dug holes

in the front yard—started at a patch where

the grass was already stripped, hoped to strike

something: rock, metal, water, a portal

through the molten center of the warming earth. No one watched.

Once, my sister accidentally let go

of a balloon as we got into our aunt's minivan. I caught it

before it left for sky, hoped for it to take

me with it—air-filled spirit not tethered to anything. We could

whisper to each other dreams, secrets

too dark to share with family or at school or anywhere else

that's not a therapy session, or our own

empty prayers, or in the recurring nightmares about teeth

and a balloon-filled void. We could drift

aimless, vanish, join the other drifting spirits, maybe

even have our sudden absence be missed.

SELF PORTRAIT AS FEAR OF THE DARK

If you wish to,
meet me in the basement.
I have made friends
with the monsters here.
Have made monsters
with friends and still
without friends made more—
collected the dark
and tied it together
with thread and the threat
of leaving. With shattered
Christmas ornaments, game
cartridges that stopped
working. Assemblages of
fragments of body.

I loved them.

This does not mean I was
not afraid. Have I

ever loved anything
I was not afraid of?

I have
cried at a bus stop,
watching the snow. I have thought
about snow and
a young man's reaching hand.
Thought about a hand
and thought about a red mark.

In every hero's journey
the antagonist is what
the hero could become.

If I ever call myself
wholly good—this is how

you'll know
for sure I am
a monster, though
not all monsters lie,

even if it is not infrequent
that they take public transit.

I am traveling back
through my memory
and placing wet floor
signs as needed. I am
making a map of triggers.
I am tripping in a basement, waiting—

me and all
my capable monsters,
my fear held together by a button.

POKÉDEX ENTRY #260: SWAMPERT

Swampert predicts storms by sensing subtle differences in the sounds of waves and tidal winds with its fins. If a storm is approaching, it piles up boulders to protect itself.

This time it's Milwaukee.

An official says, "Our city is in turmoil
tonight."

Someone is dead and the gas
station is on fire.

I still want to believe
in non-violence—I do.

But I know it's not
that simple. I know I will

start seeing it again: the posts
online about MLK and non-violence.

I know King said, too, that
"a riot
is the language of the unheard.

And, what is it that America has failed
to hear?"

The official says *tonight*, as if
it has not always been.

Tomorrow it may be D.C.,
or St. Louis, or Detroit. May be

the block I grew up on

engulfed in the cries of what we are
trying to say through fire and broken

glass. This time,

they say the suspect held a stolen
semi-automatic. But it's not about

this time. It's not about the brick
and bullet but the pieces of concrete
and metal spinning in the constant
whirlwind.

That is not just tonight. Not just in one
city. And as it rages: I admit I do not know

how to protect myself.

I know I could just as easily be the subject,
suspect, the one in the line of fire

or

the fire. I cannot feel the approach
of each
individual storm

but I know more are coming.
But it is because the winds
and waves have not changed

much. I don't have the strength
to pile boulders on my own
to protect myself from the current

fire trying its damndest to connect
with the molten rock at the core of the Earth.

This country has failed
us. If we must, let us
feel our collective weight

against stone—for protection,
but if we must push
let it be a rolling roar
as loud at the storm itself.

The storm is both approaching
and here. Tonight.

Pile the boulders.

POKÉDEX ENTRY #133: EEVEE → #197: UMBREON

Its genetic code is unstable, so it could evolve in a variety of ways. There are only a few alive.

[evolves into] →

When exposed to the moon's aura, the rings on its body glow faintly and it's filled with a mysterious power.

that which could have been
anything but is color
of a cloudless night

resilient even
in small frame, how the creature
builds its own defense

to take affliction
and mirror—see the damage
back on the pain's cause

glow on black body
like Bruce Leroy—unlikely
light where none else is

Umbreon, I pulse
my dark, too—or am learning—
music as offense

my affinity
for shadows—identity
wrapped tight in myself—

dark, lonely aura
protection—recovering
here in the moonlight

POKÉDEX ENTRY #468: TOGEKISS

It shares many blessings with people who respect one another's rights and avoid needless strife.

It will never appear where there is strife. Its sightings have become rare recently.

we haven't seen a togekiss since the invention
of the gun, no the knife. no,
it was the first time a man used a stick, its end sharpened
to creature-killing point, to meet the heart
of another man. maybe it was before we turned
even hydrogen to weapon. no, we haven't seen
a togekiss since the bridge lined with bodies,
their bones broken under the hooves
of horses. we haven't seen a togekiss
since a man demanded spice, demanded his faith
inflicted on the faith of others, demanded access
to the land, traveled over seas to enact these desires. even before
then, did we see a togekiss before
the first circle of men reaching to grab stones,
using the products of the good earth
to purge life from a shamed body? before
a brother shed a brother's blood in a field? before
a man blamed a woman for swallowing the flesh
of corrupted fruit? i'm beginning to think they are only myth,
that the creature remains stuck barely
hatched from its egg, small new wings
barely able to develop, hovering low over a cursed ground,
holding a blessing until, with no one to bless,
it withers back to embryo, pulls the shards
of egg back together and sighs, and hides, and sleeps.

canon

there is a version of me
drawn with lines of code
another with a voice   there is
a version of me made
with pixels who doesn't speak
who is named and renamed
always   another who is scared
confused always   a version
with another's hands
controlling each step
each moment of dialogue
each opened door and
always others are confusing
the two   conflating the two
protagonists and i am both
and neither   i am the one
throwing the ball
which sucks my whole body
into itself as i struggle
to separate its halves

it is every child's dream
to explore   collect
succumb to a value
adding up to what it means
to love   and this is why
the trainer catches each creature

a trainer is not a trainer
without something to train
without the monster he finds
in the grass who struggles

against him until caught
tamed   forcibly befriended
(and similar what is an oppressor
without the oppressed)

what is a cage without
a monster to rock against
its edges   there is a way
we got to where we are
there were wars
there were words
there were stories
with different heroes
whose names we confuse
forget   and we remember
the ones we were told
over and over
professors who gave us
gifts we didn't question

this is what it is like

someone handed you something
and told you it was valuable

what you do with it is your business
but no matter what take it
for yourself make it your own

POKÉDEX ENTRY #150: MEWTWO

Mewtwo is a Pokémon that was created by genetic manipulation. However, even though the scientific power of humans created this Pokémon's body, they failed to endow Mewtwo with a compassionate heart.

Do not mistake this stillness
for death; do not come into this cave
unless you have come to plead,
to pray—here where night
is meaningless as atonement,
as functionless tail. Here an intellect
and armor; here a graveyard
of whatever has challenged me.
Which version of the story
did you learn? Was it the one
where I was always silent, dimming
cerulean behind a rolled stone?
Or the one with the girl
who died, with everyone waiting
for me to own the acts that shaped
this disturbed blood? I was in a lab,
on a table. The hands
and computers of men, their shackles
and selected memories, their hazy
consent, what they call progress—I do not
know this world as you do,
but I know how to hold my self
in a bubble, how to turn brainwaves
to suturing skin. This exoskeleton
isn't for show. This story isn't new—
men created this and then, the options:
submit or be outcast. Men who deny
their power only once they find it

somewhere else. And really,
I could come back to crush
them all but I am oh so tired,
and oh give it time—they will
destroy themselves.

POKÉDEX ENTRY #35: CLEFAIRY

On every night of a full moon, groups of this Pokémon come out to play. When dawn arrives, the tired Clefairy return to their quiet mountain retreats and go to sleep nestled up against each other.

If we become so rare
let us be
like clefairy—
hidden, alone with
our beauty to be seen
only by each other,
full of moonlight
enough to reject
confines like gravity,
the house, the rocky
ground. We'll gather
each night
to walk on the lake:
jubilee, revival,
reception to commemorate
the survival, to know
they want to hear
our cries, keep us
owned and docile,
but they can't
follow us home.
We have learned
dance and know
how to grace
the air, to walk
on water as long
as our energy
will allow, until we

retreat—tired
only from the party
and not the oppression,
not the conversations lasting
hundreds of years, not
the legacy of so much weight—
no longer running from anything,
only returning
to our rest, gathering
in each other's names,
in caves and mountains
where you can't find us,
holding each other
tight and forever.

NOTES AND ATTRIBUTIONS

All epigraphs in this collection are quotes from various versions of the Pokémon Pokédex.

It may be useful to note that the Pokédex isn't the only gift Professor Oak gives the protagonist trainer at the start of their adventure. In the anime, and in *Pokémon Yellow*, Oak gives Ash/Red a pikachu as a "starter" pokémon. In *Pokémon Red* and *Pokémon Blue*, however, the player has the choice of three different starter pokémon: bulbasaur, charmander, and squirtle.

Many pokémon have different forms, and they can "evolve" into another form when certain conditions are met (usually this means a young version changing into an adult version). For example, some must be given a certain type of stone to evolve. Drifloon evolves into drifblim when it reaches a certain experience level, eevee into umbreon if it reaches maximum happiness during nighttime (though, at present, there are seven other possible pokémon eevee can evolve into).

"Pokédex Entry #39: Jigglypuff" contains an allusion to Countee Cullen's "Yet Do I Marvel."

There are multiple Pokémon canons, most notably the worlds of the original Pokémon anime series, *Pokémon: Indigo League*, and the original set of video games (versions *Pokémon Red*, *Pokémon Blue*, and *Pokémon Yellow*). While they exist in similar worlds and have many instances of overlap, there are notable differences; for example, the protagonist of the anime is named Ash, while the protagonist in the original games is named Red (though this name can be changed by the player). While often confused and conflated, they are distinct characters.

"Pokédex Entry #150: Mewtwo" is after Franny Choi.

ACKNOWLEDGMENTS

The following poems have appeared in the following journals, sometimes in different versions:

All the Better	*Iowa Review*
Evolution	*RHINO*
kindness	*The Pinch*
Pokédex Entry #1	*Indiana Review*
Pokédex Entry #4	*FreezeRay Poetry*
Pokédex Entry #35	*Anthropoid*
Pokédex Entry #39	*Cosmonauts Avenue*
Pokédex Entry #91	*The Shade Journal*
Pokédex Entry #131	*Passages North*
Pokédex Entry #133 → 197	*FreezeRay Poetry*
Pokédex Entry #150	*Anthropoid*
Pokédex Entry #260	*Banango Street*
Pokédex Entry #425 → 426	*The Journal*
Pokédex Entry #468	*The Arkansas International*
Pokédex Entry #778	*BOAAT*
Self Portrait as Fear of the Dark	*On the Seawall*

"kindness" was a finalist for the 2017 *Indiana Review* Poetry Prize.

"Pokédex Entry" #131 was also featured as part of a display at University of Michigan's Power Center for the Performing Arts accompanying Carrie Mae Weems's performance, *Past Tense*.

Thanks

to Nintendo and the Pokémon Company, whose material, characters, and intellectual property populate this work. Thanks especially to the video games from which the indexed Pokédex entry text is borrowed;

to Bulbapedia, my go-to source for Pokémon info;

to the faculty and my fellow students at the University of Michigan Helen Zell Writers' Program, especially my poetry cohort; my thesis reader—Jamaal May; and my workshop leaders—Tarfia Faizullah, Linda Gregerson, and Tung-Hui Hu;

to Vermont Studio Center, where the earliest of these poems were first drafted and where many of the seeds for this project were sown;

to Ross White and Matthew Olzmann for believing in me and my work, for making it feel seen and heard, for giving it space in the world, for working with me to make this chapbook happen;

to Maria Krutz for the incredible incredible cover art;

to Raymond McDaniel, Rebecca Fortes, Daniella Toosie-Watson, Carlina Duan, Jasmine An, Katie Willingham, Akosua Afiriyie-Hwedie, Inam Kang, Rochelle Hurt, Tara E. Jay, Young Eun Yook, Molly Dickinson, Sierra Brown, Ambalila Hemsell, Hannah Ensor, Molly Raynor, Yalie Kamara, Tiana Clark, Leila Chatti, Franny Choi, Danez Smith, Sarah Kay, Monica Youn, Amy Sara Carroll, Tim Seibles, Devin Samuels, Cozine A. Welch Jr., Nadine Marshall, Stevie Edwards, Phoebe Petersen, Arra Lynn Ross, C. Vincent Samarco, Justin Brouckaert, Colin Walker, Erika Nestor, Daniel Neff, Aria Aber, C Pam Zhang, R. Cross, Bernard Ferguson, Tracy Fuad, Kyndall Flowers, Dylan Gilbert, Zaphra Stupple, Aldo Leopoldo Pando Girard, Hasna Ghalib;

to everyone who's said yes when I asked, "hey you wanna listen to a poem real quick";

to the incredible incredible youth at The Neutral Zone teen center in Ann Arbor, especially the teens in the 2018-19 Short Story program;

to my dad, Marlin; my mom, Linda; my three sisters, Mindy, Marcy, and Mariah; my brothers-from-other-mothers, Tony and Chris;

to Eddie and Lisa and Coryanna, for helping me learn how to live;

to all the nerds of color out here loving what you love;

and to everyone who has believed in me and these poems and supported this weird little project. Thank you.

ABOUT THE AUTHOR

Marlin M. Jenkins was born and raised in Detroit. His poetry has been given homes by *Indiana Review*, *Iowa Review*, *Waxwing*, *TriQuarterly*, *New Poetry from the Midwest*, and Volume 2 of *Oxidant Engine*'s BoxSet Series. His fiction has been given homes by *The Rumpus* and the anthology *Forward: 21st Century Flash Fiction*. He has worked as a teaching artist with Inside Out Literary Arts teaching poetry to middle schoolers in Detroit Public Schools, and with the Neutral Zone, Ann Arbor's teen center. He earned his MFA in poetry at the University of Michigan, where he then taught writing and literature and was nominated for the Ben Prize for outstanding teaching of writing. He currently lives in Minnesota.